Introduction

Denise Gebhart

Art remains a constant element of life. Whether fine arts, performing arts, literature, or design, we are permanently surrounded by art. It plays such an important role in human life and human identity that a world without art would be unthinkable.

Because each work of art is unique and opens up different perspectives, it helps us to define ourselves and find our place in society. While artists try to convey a certain meaning through their work, beholders attempt to interpret and enjoy it.

The beholder often sees only the artwork and not the person behind it. We decided to move away from the position of mere beholder and take a look at the actual lives of artists and the ways they work. On the following pages, you will find interviews with contemporary artists from around the globe. The artists reveal insights about their lives, experiences, and inspirations. Seeing a more personal side of the creator shines a different light on the creation.

The Interviews

Hanna Al-khouli spoke with Sebastian Sanders. Sanders, originally from The Netherlands, has made his way in the art world step by step. He currently lives and works in Oslo, Norway, and is involved with art scenography, using sculptures and photography to create illusions and optical effects. Stefanie Svacina edited the interview with Sanders and also held an interview with Afroditi Psarra, a Greek artist who led a workshop at the University of Salzburg. Among other things, Psarra's workshops teach participants how to transform a coil sewn into material into a loud speaker. And this is actually what Psarra's art is about: combining technology and art to produce so-called e-textiles; fabrics equipped with electronic devices to produce lights and movement and sound. Psarra participates in exhibitions, workshops, and festivals throughout the world and is at the cutting edge of wearable technology.

Stefanie Niesner and Christina König spoke with another technology aficionado, Greger Stolt Nilsen, who is based in Oslo, Norway. Stolt Nilsen, a software programmer by day, is a dedicated artist who uses his technical skills to create art that is inspired by the events of everyday life.

Jana Winkelmayer skyped with Andrew McDonald who lives and works in London, United Kingdom. McDonald, originally from rural New Zealand, is not only a performer, but also works in textile design, sculpture, and painting and has held exhibitions on many continents.

A group of three students, Ilse Huber-Craigher, Jessica Weber, and Sabine Pusswald were able to connect with the final interview partner, Charlotte Eckler, who is based in Grafton, Massachusetts. Eckler, a conceptual artist originally from Los Angeles, California, works with prints, collages, fabrics, and paintings, and includes social critique and political statement in her art.

Denise Gebhart is a master's student living and working in Salzburg, Austria. After completing a bachelor's degree in Korean studies at the University of Vienna, she began her master's in comparative literature and culture at the University of Salzburg. She also teaches Korean at the adult education center in Salzburg.

SEBASTIAN SANDERS

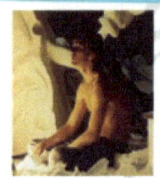

HANNA AL-KHOULI

I AM WHERE I AM,
AND THIS IS WHO I AM

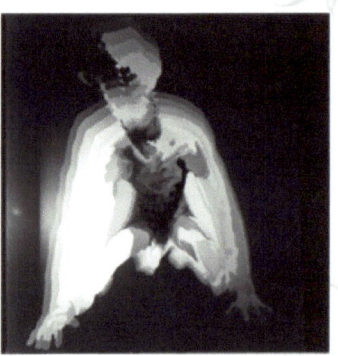

RESONANCE/1998/

"I am where I am, and this is who I am"

Sebastian Sanders in conversation with **Hanna Al-khouli**

Compiled by Stefanie Svacina

Dutch artist **Sebastian Sanders** makes people "learn to read, to use their eyes." Sanders, who lives and works in Oslo, Norway, achieves this by working with illusions and optical effects, craftsmanship and experimenting.

In an interview with Hanna Al-Khouli, Sanders offers insight into his life, his career, and his art. He not only discusses ways to approach contemporary art, but also how certain decisions can change the path of your life. As Sanders says, "Every step you take in your life has a consequence."

What is your art about?

It is about illusions and creating spatial depths. For example, I often work at night with layers ... forcing people to focus with their eyes. If you have several layers, people will look at the front, and their eyes have to focus forwards and backwards. The public has to actually read the piece. Making people learn to read and use their eyes, that is the content of my work.

What inspires you?

If you look at the wireframe pieces, which are these things made of wooden sticks, they're very much based in the early 1990s. Computers were coming out and everyone was getting more into the computer world so when all the commercials came out, they were into this wireframe imaging and that was the hottest stuff ... I decided to bring this back by adding a personal touch, and by using wood and making line contour drawings of 3-D objects. They are a comment of sorts on the computer-generated wireframe world, but with a personal touch added on.

How do you start your work and how do you know you are finished?

I think with most artists it is a process: One thing leads to another. ... I enjoy working with illusions and optical effects, and I use a lot of craftsmanship and experiments. If you look at the *Resonance* piece—one of my earlier works—it is basically made of a clay figure. I cut the figure into several pieces, traced around the body, and then cut layers in paper and hung them one after the other. What happened then was that a person with a lamp walked by and I suddenly saw the effect: The light can move! I tried to think what would work... I mean, if you are going to cut paper, cut holes in the paper and you are trying to get the tonality of lights on the blank surfaces—what image should you use? I could do an image of a horse or a banana or whatever, but in this case [in the *Resonance* piece], the movement reminded me of driving on the highway at night and the lights in tunnels that go "brrr brrr."

When is the piece finished? I think, if you are making paintings, it is a lot easier to stop at a certain point, but my pieces need to have openness...

Who discovered you, or what triggered your career as an artist?

What happened with me was... Well, I was studying in Holland, when I met a Norwegian girl and we fell madly in love. We traveled through South America for a long time. Then it was my turn to move to Norway for one year, where I did my master's degree at the art academy. Then a gallery picked me up. If that had not happened, I would not still be in Norway, and I would not have gotten to where I am now.

I did a couple of shows abroad with this gallery but I had great difficulties communicating with [the gallerist] because he doesn't think like an artist; he is more of a businessman. This was very frustrating for me as he wanted me to produce five pieces of the same work. So, I got a little bit disappointed and moved away from this to make more personal art. Now, I am involved in producing works for theaters and things like that.

Did you organize your life to become an artist, or did it come peu à peu?

It is a process, and of course you have to plan things in life. What do you want to do? Where do you want to go? What are your goals in life? Those things... It is really difficult to just say, "Okay, I want to be a stock broker or a doctor." I mean, when you are a teenager you think, "I want to be an astronaut or travel the world." Then, at some point, you decide to become more realistic and you start to find out what you are good at. You begin to focus more on that.

Did you ever picture yourself in this position in life?

Interesting question... I think, what you are asking is, if I thought I would ever become an artist? [...] Every step you take in your life has a consequence. I never thought I would be living in Norway. I came here for just one year ... and now I have been living here for eighteen years. So, what happened with me: I studied art history for ... one and a half years, and I was very interested in the arts but I got so depressed with studying art history. What has happened now, I am moving more from the actual production of my own pieces, and am concentrating more on art scenography and pieces for theaters. So, I do not know where I will end up.

Do you feel good about what you are doing, or do you want to change something about your life?

At this stage of life in my forties, I am where I am and this is who I am. I think, every human being is thinking of a higher level, but the art-life is not easy. It is not big money all the time, but, I guess, I am pretty satisfied with who I am. I have to fix my car because it is broken now, so naturally I would like to have more money—but I am happy with who I am.

Hanna Al-khouli is an emerging designer, and architect, and new to Salzburg. He is originally from Syria.

AFRODITI PSARRA

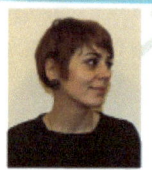

STEFANIE SVACINA

AFRODITI PSARRA
AND HER EXTREMES

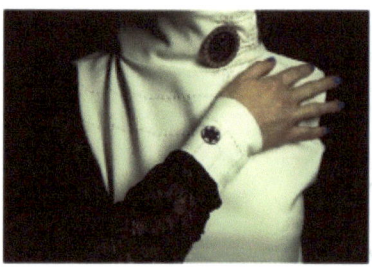

IDORU /2013/

Afroditi Psarra and Her Extremes

Stefanie Svacina

The multidisciplinary Greek artist **Afroditi Psarra**, born in 1982, is a woman of contradictions: Initially a painter, she soon became more interested in coding; continuing to work with traditional folk art, she nonetheless combines her art with new technologies; and working with soft fabrics, she sews in solid electronics. In short, she specializes in e-textiles.

Psarra has been interested in both art and technology for most of her life. By the age of ten she had learned how to program as part of her extracurricular activities at school. For her university studies, however, Psarra chose fine arts. As a painter, she undertook classical artistic training while still maintaining her interest in technology. After obtaining her bachelor's degree, she felt that there had already been enough said about the arts throughout the centuries, so she switched her major in order to combine her interests.

Today, Psarra holds a PhD in Image, Technology, and Design, which she obtained from Complutense University in Madrid, Spain. Now a renowned artist, she contributes to residency programs throughout Europe and participates in international festivals, exhibitions, and workshops. Most recently, Psarra took part in the AST 2015—Art Science Technology festival in Grenoble, France—where she performed Soft^Articulations, a sound performance that translates the articulations of muscles into sounds. For this performance, the artist used so-called e-textiles.

E-textiles are modified fabrics amplified with electronic devices in order to create a unique and technical artifact. In her work, Psarra transforms fabrics into futuristic body wear that produces sounds or triggers movements, bringing to mind the fashion of science fiction films. Asking why she uses fabrics rather than the human body as a medium, she explains:

"I am really interested in the fabric itself because it kind of combines this soft quality, and, with the electronics, it juxtaposes this softness with the hardness of the electronics or with the hardness of the sound. [...] Also, it is a kind of medium to create sudden technological development that can be more integrated into everyday life and into tradition..., because textiles are closely related to tradition and folk art."

Psarra creates e-textiles, which—in their production process—are closely interwoven with tradition. For her, the crucial element is the fabric itself, which wraps around the human body. By adding electronic devices, the fabric further develops into a new and—to a certain degree—independent organism. The artist not only creates new art pieces, but also performs with them. Her performances are mostly sound performances without any specific choreography; instead, she improvises her movements to illustrate the variety of sounds produced by combining cloths and electronics.

During her studies in the field of e-textiles, Psarra met many colleagues whom she admires. Whilst her favorite artist as a teenager was Keith Haring, she now looks up to the Russian duo Dmitry Gelfand and Evelina Domnitch who combine the world of physics and chemistry to create art. Furthermore, Psarra is inspired by Ebru Kurbak and the collective Kobakant (Mika Satomi and Hannah Perner-Wilson) who, like Psarra, work with e-textiles, new technologies, and the human body. Notably, these artists work together on many projects to develop new ideas and support each other with their knowledge.

Psarra also benefits from these collaborations, although she is used to working alone. Still, she admits that sometimes she, too, needs help. "When [there is] a project that is very technical and requires, I don't know, programming skills that I don't have, or kind of more elaborated sound for work that I actually produce, I collaborate with other people." Nonetheless, Psarra is an all-rounder. She not only produces innovative pieces of art and is a natural talent in programming; she can also adapt herself to the specific environment in which she is working and has no problem working together in spaces with others. During her residency programs, she learned to stay focused no matter where she was; but at home she can still be distracted, and prefers a quiet space with lots of room to lay out her materials and tools.

Psarra does not simply sit back and enjoy her success. She loves challenges and seeks new ideas and input whenever and wherever possible. She points out that her ideas originate from "any sort of source of inspiration," from reading a novel, watching a play or movie, or reading someone's thesis. When something catches her attention, she conducts research to establish a prototype. Her art is finished, as she says, when she is pleased with it—which might be difficult ... as she admits to being a perfectionist. With regard to herself, she says, "I think I am the worst critic, I am really hard on myself. Always."

Psarra remains true to herself and focuses on what is important in her life, namely, art and technology. Although she began her career as a painter, she has found a way to combine her interests in the best way possible—e-textiles. Psarra is an artist of the future confronting folk art with new technology, and textiles with electronics, which allows tradition to continue in new ways and forms.

Stefanie Svacina is a freelance museum docent and art historian who lives and works in Salzburg. She is currently writing her master's thesis on the Fourth Plinth, a display for contemporary sculptures at Trafalgar Square in London.

GREGER STOLT NILSEN

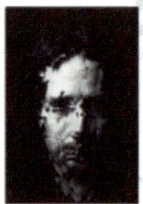

STEFANIE NIESNER
CHRISTINA KÖNIG

THE ART IN PLAYING
SOLITAIRE

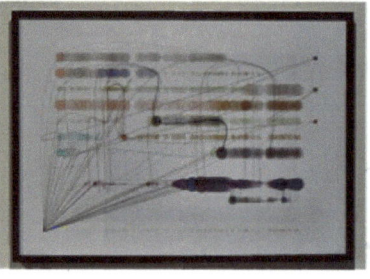

WASTED/2008/

The Art in Playing Solitaire

Gregor Stolt Nilsen in conversation with **Christina König and Stefanie Niesner**

*Meet **Greger Stolt Nilsen**, a graduate from the Trondheim Academy of Fine Arts. By day, he writes software programs for newspapers; but by night, he uses his computer skills for his life-long passion: art. In our interview, he talks about how inspiring a doctor's appointment can be, what being an artist has to do with saying "I love you," and the poetry of chat messages.*

Hi Greger, thank you so much for taking the time for this interview. Our first question: How do you start your work and when do you know you're finished?

That's very hard to answer. Sometimes an idea just pops into my mind or I simply sit down, start writing program codes, and see where that takes me. I usually know my work is finished when I exhibit it or use it for an application.

Or you let a computer decide—in one of your projects from 2010, "Computer-Assisted Painting," you write a code that lets the computer decide what the picture looks like and when it's finished.

Yes, that's right. In this case, I didn't get to choose how the picture looks. The program did that for me. I only wrote the code and painted whatever it showed me. It calculated how much black should be in the picture and as soon as there was enough, it told me to stop. Also, I didn't know beforehand how long I would spend on each of these pictures.

What atmosphere do you like to work in? What do you find distracting?

I can work almost anywhere as long as I have my laptop, but I also have my own studio. I'd like it to be tidy, but it almost never is. So the most distracting thing is not having the things I need— and other people. (*laughs*)

What inspires you?

Anything; a word, a sentence, a feeling. One day, I was at the doctor's office and heard one of the secretaries say to a patient, "What's the matter with you?" Somehow that stuck with me and ended up in one of my projects. On another day, I was sitting in my studio, playing Solitaire over and over again, procrastinating; after a while I became very conscious of the angry mouse moves I made, so I modified the software to log all of them and turn them into graphics. Inspiration comes from anywhere, I guess.

When did you first call yourself an artist?

That was only after I went to the art academy, after I got my bachelor's degree. I remember it being hard in the beginning—it's a bit like telling someone you love them for the first time—it sounds so cheesy at first, but after you do it for a while, it becomes natural. And I figured, since I had my bachelor's degree, it was justified—I had the certificate to prove it. (*laughs*)

How do you handle criticism?

I love it. Good criticism can really help you and it's fascinating to see what other people make of your art. But of course it depends on where it's coming from and what kind of criticism it is. I don't criticize how a car mechanic does his job, either.... Or if someone just tells me, "you suck," then I generally ignore it.

On a little more personal note: On a scale from one to ten, how good of a friend are you?

Six, maybe? My problem is that I rarely see my friends. Most of the time, I'm at work or at my studio, and the little time I have left, I like to just relax and do nothing. But when we do hang out, I believe I'm a good friend. Even better than six.

To get back to your work: You once made a book with all the chat messages you sent in a year, in alphabetical order. What's the meaning behind this?

I liked the absurdity of sentences that are taken out of context. They make no sense by themselves, and at the same time, you get a lot of random connections between them, which can be quite funny. You put together masses of sentences and somehow their meaning changes; they become more (or less) than they originally were. The project also turned into a study of myself and I often caught myself thinking, "Oh no, this is going to be in a book, I can't say it like this." It was like publishing my journal, in a way.

Isn't it a warning that everything we say online can be recorded and put in another context – one that was not intended?

It can be seen like that, of course, but that wasn't my initial idea.

Does it bother you when people interpret your work differently than you would?

Not at all. I actually prefer it if people make up their own minds about my work. I can't make them see something that isn't there for them, and that's okay. The best that can happen is that my art poses a question. Good art should always ask questions and not just tell you something.

Last, but not least: Are you angry?

If I am angry? *(laughs)* Some people would call me that, but no, I don't think I'm angry. I do get annoyed easily, especially by other people. I don't really like hanging out with people I don't know, doing small talk, things like that. I tend to avoid that and would rather be with my friends or by myself.

Thank you very much.

Christina König was born 1993 in Linz. After finishing her bachelor's degree in German Philology, she began her current studies of Comparative Literature and Cultural Studies in Salzburg.

Stefanie Niesner, born 1991 in Gmunden, Austria is finishing her bachelor's degree in history in summer 2016.

ANDREW McDONALD

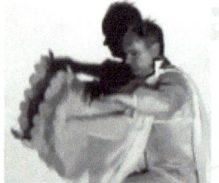

JANA WINKELMAYER

HOW IT FEELS TO BE
A HUMAN BEING ALIVE TODAY

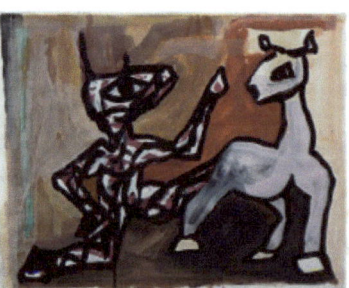

UNTITLED /2013/

"How it Feels to be a Human Being Alive Today"

Jana Winkelmayer

"I am running late," **Andrew McDonald** tells me and just as I start to assume he is in a hurry, he politely adds, "I just hope that I am awake and with you." We have a video conference. He is sitting in front of a huge bookshelf, seeming relaxed and in tune with himself. Originally from New Zealand, McDonald now lives and works in London. Many of his performances are held there in his studio. In the video footage I watched in preparation for the interview, the ambience of the small courtyard seemed quite intimate.

It is a group studio, so there are always people around. McDonald admits that the random input he gets is a valuable source for his compositions. "Otherwise you can become too involved in your own work. [...] Other people obviously give you a different perspective," he adds. I want to know what atmosphere he finds best to be creative in and McDonald is direct in telling me that his studio is a bit messy, full of paintings and costumes. Those items don't disturb him, but other than music, he tries to reduce distractions as much as possible.

Since he works in London, there is always lots of noise. McDonald has been living in the city since 1986 and completed his Master of Arts in Millinery Design at the *Royal College of Art.* He did not continue working as a milliner but instead developed his skills in a broad range of textile design, paintings, sculptures, and performances. McDonald has held exhibitions throughout the world and has been actively involved in London's art scene since the mid-1980s.

So, how does someone who elaborated so many different fields of art usually start his work? Especially when it comes to performances, the "making of" is always a slow process over a long period of time. I find out, that McDonald lays the foundation for his diverse spectrum of production in the early stages of his work. He gathers his ideas from very different places, and collects material in abstract and manifest ways. Sometimes even before starting with an idea. After a while he begins to write them down or captures them in paintings. In the same way costumes are carefully prepared. Only when he paints, he seems to let go of control, being driven by a more spontaneous force. He then just pops his ideas out and sees what will happen later. Sometimes he takes it from there, other times he has to adjust the outcome. Anyway, his approach is always light-hearted and experimental.

His work comprises both finding out what a work means to him, and what it means to other people. Depending on his viewers' individual experiences, they fill the blank spaces with their own memories. McDonald is an artist who encourages this process. Finding out what his work means to him is a lifelong task and changes over time. To him, painting his pictures is like its own language. Combing through McDonald's paintings the attentive observer will come across a devilish figure with horns on the head. This figure can be compared to a word that occurs over and over again. It functions as a symbol for feeling positive and having an open, powerful attitude when facing the future.

One will also notice that McDonald seems consumed by visions of different heads. "Why heads?" I ask curiously and get a surprisingly easy answer: The origin lies in his millinery education. When all the other students were complaining about the detailed work, McDonald actually liked it a lot. He grew fond of the idea of contributing to the perpetuation of a dying art. Later, he started to realize that what he really was interested in was not the work as a milliner, but the heads themselves. So he began the process of making his passion his profession. For McDonald, the head is where the personality is located. By adding certain accessories, the perception can be easily manipulated. To focus purely on this part of the body provides the opportunity to free the evolved personality from society's attributions and its identity in general.

Who is looking at whom?

A performance's main aim is always to make people watch. In the piece "Who is looking?" McDonald walks around, dressed in a self-made, colorful and eccentric costume. His fake long hair is tied up in a ponytail. Suddenly he turns around and takes photos of the audience watching him. McDonald is trying to get attention. Not only is he dressed differently but he also uses stylized gestures. By trying to capture the moment for himself, he ends up turning tables. "Our first response to something is to record it for later. So rather than necessarily being completely present at the moment, we want to kind of take it away with us." The questioning of gender and sexuality, which is present in "Who is looking?" is a fundamental part of McDonald's work. He longs to free his costumes even from queer designing traditions. He is searching for the ultimate screen on which the viewer is invited to project new concepts.

Being part of controversial debates always leads to intense reactions. People do not always have the decency to communicate their point of view in a manner that is free of emotion and affect. The anonymity of the internet can reinforce this.

McDonald tells me with a slightly surprised but still pleased smile that he has finally entered the world of social media. His work thus enters realms where people who have not necessarily sought it out, are affected by it. He admits that criticism can disturb how you think. To him it is much easier to stay unaffected, if you have no close relationship to the person who addresses you. "It is not a pleasant process, but a good one. [...] It keeps you challenging yourself because you are being challenged,"

McDonald describes feedback as a valuable and helpful opportunity to bring unaware aspects of your work to the surface.

When I ask him to rate himself on a scale from one to ten considering how good of a friend he is, McDonald gives himself an eight. He likes to think that he is a good friend, but it is hard for him to decide. I ask him about his driving force in life and it takes him a while to name it. In the end, he sticks to the term "art" and defines it as "the expression of how it feels to be a human being alive today." There are certain things about life and the world that make him angry. Especially injustice or the way that people can be judgmental and filled with hatred towards others at times.

I can imagine how a sensitive and open person like him is touched by negativity and unawareness. Earlier in the interview I came up with the old question if the glass is half empty or half full, and found out that to him it really depends on the day. When we finish our interview I notice how easy and comfortable it was talking to him. Time has flown by fast and I wish him a great rest of the day. "I will try to make sure the glass is half full," he answers laughing.

Jana Winkelmayer is a freelance journalist and writer living and working in Vienna. She completed a Bachelor's of Theater-, Film- and Media Sciences and is now in the masters program for comparative literature and cultural studies at the University of Salzburg. She is currently working on her master's thesis about identity formation and the staging of the human body.

CHARLOTTE ECKLER

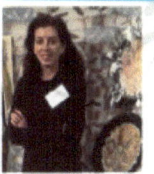

JESSICA WEBER
SABINE PUSSWALD
ILSE HUBER-CRAIGHER

MEANINGFUL MESSAGES
AND FILTERED NEWS

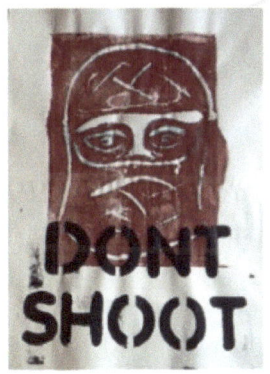

HANDS UP/DON'T SHOOT
/2014/

Meaningful Messages and Filtered News

Ilse Huber Craigher, Sabine Pusswald, and **Jessica Maria Weber**

"There's a higher purpose to what I'm trying to say, and that purpose is to make a point, socially."

For **Charlotte Eckler**, U.S.-American conceptual artist, delivering a meaningful message to the public is the goal she wants to achieve with her art. Police brutality, racism, feminism, war, sickness, are all present as topics in Eckler's work. Whether she's working with prints, collages, fabrics, or paintings, she always finds a way to weave in her political opinion.

Hands Up / Don't Shoot is the name of one of her projects, a slogan she borrowed from the demonstrations in Ferguson, U.S. after the shooting of the African-American Michael Brown by a white police officer. This large installation piece made of wood and hardware, covered with silkscreen prints, drawings, and fiber art among other things, is a nod to the protests against police brutality as well as a historical reference to the feminist movement.

As a woman artist Eckler is very aware of gender inequality and everything that comes with it, although personally, she has never experienced gender discrimination at art shows. She has been able to steer clear of it, in part, by participating in shows where only women were involved. "So automatically, I was shielded from discrimination," Eckler explains.

Another socially and political relevant topic that she focuses on is war. She refers to war in many of her prints, not only to actual war zones, but also to the domestic war against people of color in the U.S. The most recent group show that she participated in bore the title *War and Peace*. Eckler's contribution was an installation of a public poster column of the kind used in Europe since the nineteenth century to announce events. Eckler made a collage of sorts on these columns, printing onto World War II headlines from the *New York Times* as well as mythological stories. As the installation is interactive, people can step inside and write something on a paper roll, therefore becoming part of the art piece. Her goal is to raise public awareness and promote freedom of speech away from censorship. Her piece can also be regarded as a counterpart to the mainstream media coverage since, as she states: "In the United States, the news is filtered. Everything's filtered. You don´t know what´s going on. You can only guess by trying to see the larger picture, going back in history, and looking for what repeats itself."

Despite being influenced by these negative events, Eckler doesn't appear to be an angry or frustrated person. When asked about precisely that, she laughs it off, but still admits, "There are certain things I get angry about. I get angry at injustice."

Two points are crucial in her working process: time and space to work. Naturally, one needs material to work with, but Eckler seems able to go with the flow and turn an idea into an artwork with the materials she has on hand. However, when planning a long-

term piece, "sometimes it's an impediment if you have to go and buy things to even start the artwork. You have to think, 'What's gonna be the right material? What's gonna work?' What's available?'"

In response to the question of how she knows when she's finished with a piece of art, or the right moment to stop, Eckler simply says, "You have to say to yourself, 'It's done. I don't have anything to add.'" That seems to be a problem with many artists—finding the moment when something is finished. Eckler also knows about this fragile moment of completion, which is why she recommends working in different media. For example, when working on a computer, every step can be reversed.

"Some people have an equivalent of writer's block with art," Eckler says. That is a problem she does not have. For her, the most important thing about creating art is that "you have to do it ... yourself." If you do that, Eckler explains, and if you don't lose sight of the higher goal you've set for yourself, you won't be bothered much by criticism. After all, inspiration is never too far away. All you have to do is go through life with your eyes wide open.

Ilse Huber Craigher, Mag.Phil, a retired teacher, lives and works as an artist in Salzburg (Austria)

Sabine Pusswald lives and works in Salzburg. She is currently pursuing a master's degree in comparative literature and cultural studies at the University of Salzburg. In 2012, she completed her bachelor's degree in communication studies at the University of Vienna. She has also gathered a great deal of experience working in journalism and public relations over the course of the last few years.

Jessica Maria Weber grew up in the state of Bavaria in Germany and is currently located in Salzburg, Austria. She is a communications science major and also takes classes that are compelling and important to her. Weber doesn't like so-called experts for every form of art to tell her what's "right," "beautiful," and "expressive," etc. She prefers to be carried away by the mood and the pieces and loves to be swept off her feet by *duende* (the mysterious power of art to deeply move a person). In her opinion, life has to be lived with passion and awareness; the two forces that keep her going.

This publication resulted from a project in the course "Talking and Writing about Art" taught by Lisa Rosenblatt, held jointly by the University of Salzburg and the Mozarteum. We are grateful for the financial support from the Program Area Contemporary Art and Cultural Production (Focus Area Humanities & Art.

Thanks go to Hanna Al-khouli for the design of this publication and to all the students and interviewees for their time and insight.

February 2016